T0354888

FOREWARD

"Chosen", the book written by Pastor Barbara M. Smith, is truly a Spirit-filled work inspired by the Holy Ghost. The passages are filled with uplifting encouragements that help oppressed and depressed believers that face the trials and tribulations of the faith walk. The book is filled with kingdom living principles that allow the believer to filter through the dark clouds of doubt and unbelief and look through to a clear glass of hope. I expect that this work will readily grip its readers and maintain one's interest to the very end. It is a bull's –eye account of a believer's walk with Chris and it abounds with truth and hope in its accounts.

Judge Brenda Sanders.

CHOSEN.....

Dr. Barbara M. Smith, PhD

Order this book online at www.trafford.com
or email orders@trafford.com

Most Trafford titles are also available at major online book retailers.

Note for Librarians: A cataloguing record for this book is available from Library and Archives Canada at www.collectionscanada.ca/amicus/index-e.html

Printed in Victoria, BC, Canada.

ISBN: 978-1-4269-1872-8 (sc)

Our mission is to efficiently provide the world's finest, most comprehensive book publishing service, enabling every author to experience success. To find out how to publish your book, your way, and have it available worldwide, visit us online at www.trafford.com

Trafford rev. 11/14/2009

People's names and certain details mentioned in this book have been changed to protect the privacy of the individuals involved. However, the essence of what happened and the underlying principles have been conveyed as accurately as possible.

 www.trafford.com

North America & international
toll-free: 1 888 232 4444 (USA & Canada)
phone: 250 383 6864 ♦ fax: 812 355 4082

DEDICATION

This book is dedicated to the most wonderful man I have ever met, my precious, loving husband, Deacon Frederick Lee Smith. Because of your patience and encouragement, I was able to complete this book.

To my two children: Frederick L. Smith Jr. and Kristen Joi Smith. Thank you, for allowing me to fulfill God's will for my life. You are my greatest blessings from God. You are blessed and God is going to use you both in a great way some day.

ACKNOWLEDGMENTS

If I were to acknowledge all the special people who have contributed to my life and to the success of this project, the list of names would be too lengthy to record. I have learned from everyone who has been a part of my life, and to them I offer my thanks and appreciation. I deeply appreciate the following individuals for their encouragement while writing this book:

My parents, Henry C. Jenkins and Barbara M. Jenkins
My sister, Pastor Karen Michelle Wasson
Minister Yvette Denison
Minister Kay Brundage
Minister Brenda K. Saunders
Dr. Wendell Scales, DDS
My editor: Pastor Simon Presland

Words cannot express my gratitude for the wisdom and mentoring I have received from the most profound preachers of today, who have sown seeds of greatness in my life:

Rev. Dr. Valmon D. Stotts
Pastor Benard D. Holcomb
Pastor Eugene Matthews
Rev. Dr. Edgar L. Vann
Drs. Tony & Regina Patrick
Mrs. Emily (Tolbert) Holt

Finally, I give God the highest praise and thank the Holy Spirit for his teaching and guidance in the writing of this book.

Father, thank you for bringing your vision for my life to pass.

Contents

FORWARD

When the Lord calls or chooses us for his purposes we feel we are ready and fully equipped to go forth in our calling at that particular time. However, that is rarely the case. We must all go through a preparation period. Although the Lord has a plan and purpose for all of his people, unless we go through a training period, we will not be able to handle the situations that arise as we work in our ministries. For example, consider King Saul and King David in 1 Samuel. Both were anointed by the prophet Samuel to be king over Israel. However, Saul's character was still of the "flesh" while David's was of the "spirit." When Saul's training periods arose in his life—the trials and temptations he faced—he hid from them. David, on the other hand, faced his life's trials and by the time he became king, he was humble and useful to God.

Similarly, we must go through our own training period—the tests as well as the situations we face in life in relation to our heart, character, and Jesus' Lordship in our lives—in order to walk in the calling God has for us. The Lord must take us through a refining process in order to align our way of thinking to his.

"Let this mind be in you, which was also in Christ Jesus" (Philippians 2:5).

Rejection, lack of self confidence, self limitation, and impatience are a few of the issues the Lord must address so new can participate in building his kingdom.

The purpose of this book is to help you understand that no matter what you have gone through in the past or must face in the future, the Word of God states He will never leave you or forsake you (Hebrews 13:5). He will be by your side during your wilderness experience. Like Jesus, our Heavenly Father wants to bring us forth in the power of His Spirit. Jesus had to go through a wilderness experience before He went into His earthly ministry.

"For I know the thoughts that I think toward you, saith the Lord, thoughts of peace, and not of evil, to give you and expected end" (Jeremiah 9:11).

You can rest assured that when your training is complete you will be well prepared to go forth to fulfill your purposes in the power and the anointing of God.

CHAPTER 1 - LIFE'S EXPERIENCES - SALVATION

Life can be quite challenging. It can bring about some wonderful experiences as well as earth shattering ones. Sometimes our circumstances are so fulfilling, we want to shout for joy. At other times, they can get so rough; we almost despair of life itself. There comes a point where we realize we can't handle all of our circumstances. The Word tells us, "man that is born of a woman is of few days, and full of trouble."[1] After going through several bad situations, we begin to realize we won't survive if we don't get help. The blessing is that our Heavenly Father will send people into our lives to show us that our troubles are rooted in the fact that we are sinners in need of a Savior. Through these people, the Lord will show us that Jesus is the only one who can save us, get us through life safely, and bless us in the life to come.

After we have been made aware that all who call upon the name of the Lord shall be saved, we must confess with our mouth the Lord Jesus, and believe in our heart that God has raised him from the dead we then become saved individuals, Christians, children of the Great High King.[2] The word states, "if any man be in Christ (saved), he is a new creature: old things are passed away; behold all things are become new."[3]

We as Christians are to live changed lives. We are not to live as the people of this world live any longer. In fact Romans 12:1-2 tells us we are to present our bodies as a living sacrifice, holy and acceptable unto God, which is our reasonable service.[4] Instead of conforming to this world, we are to be transformed by the renewing of our minds.

It is for these reasons the Lord takes us through basic training in relation to how His kingdom operates. He teaches us how to pray, praise, worship, fast, about spiritual warfare, and so much more. These experiences help God to transform and shape our life into the image and likeness of Christ.

While you are learning the basics of Christianity, the Lord will have you work in different areas in the church. And if you ask Him, He will show you why He put you here on earth. He will show you his purpose in creating you.

The Call

Let's talk about being *called or chosen* of God. To be *called* according to the Webster's Dictionary means to "give the order, to bring into action, to manage by giving the signal or orders." To be *chosen* means one has been "selected or marked for favor or special privilege, to be distinguished by some unusual quality from others of the same category."

The following scriptures tell us God's idea of being called and chosen:

Ye have not chosen me, but I have chosen you, and ordained you, that ye should go and bring forth fruit, and that your fruit should remain: that what so ever ye shall ask of the father in my name, he may give it to you (John 15:16).

So the first shall be last, and the first last, for many be called, but few chosen (Matthew 20:16).

To whom coming, as unto a living stone, disallow indeed of men, but chosen of God and precious.[5]

Before I formed thee in the belly, I knew the: and before thou camest forth out of the womb I sanctified thee, and I ordained thee a prophet unto the nations.[6]

According as he hath chosen as in him before the foundation of the world, that we should be holy and without blame before him in love.[7]

But ye are a chosen generation, a royal priesthood, an holy nation, a peculiar people, that ye should shew praises of him who hath called you out of darkness into his marvelous light.[8]

You might be wondering why God has the right to make choices. The answer is found in Psalms 24:1-2 "the earth is the Lords and the fullness there of, the world and they that dwell therein. For he founded it upon the seas, and established it upon the floods."[9]

It is evident God created every thing and everyone. As Creator, He has the right to make decisions in relation to his creation. He is sovereign: He can do whatever He wants, whenever He wants to.

God has called and chosen His prospective leaders since the beginning of time. He chose Moses to lead the Israelites out of bondage from Egypt. He chose Abraham to be the father of many nations. He chose David to become Israel's greatest king and ancestor of Jesus Christ. Esther was chosen by God to approach the king on behalf of her people. He chose Debra to be judge over Israel. He chose Isaiah to be a prophet in Israel. It was God's choice that Saul be transformed from a persecutor of Christians to a preacher for Christ. In every instance, God's choices were his alone. They were not imposed upon Him out of necessity, and they conformed to His will.

God's choices are internally motivated. They are acts of love. The explanation for God's choices must be sought in the character of God, and not in any quality of the individuals chosen. God decides who He wants to use and how He wants to use them. It is not because of our goodness that he chooses us, He simply exercises his sovereignty.

If you study the Word of God, you will discover that the people I have just mentioned were called in different ways. You might not be called to preach the word, but whatever your calling, your service is needed in the Body of Christ.

> Wherefore he saith, when He ascended up on high, he led captivity captive, and gave gifts unto men. And he gave some apostles, and some prophets, and some, evangelists; and some, pastors and some teachers; for the perfecting of the saints, for the work of the ministry, for the edifying of the body of Christ: Till we all come in the unity of the faith, and of the knowledge of the Son of God, unto a perfect man, unto the measure of the stature of the fullness of Christ.
>
> Ephesians 4:8,11-13

So don't get hung up on the call. Before I received the call to preach, I taught the Word in churches, in prisons, in nursing homes, and in seminars. I was excited about all of my assignments because serving the Lord is an honor and a privilege. It is a blessing to be able to teach His Word. I loved teaching so much that I taught every time the Lord opened a door for me.

"Thy word is a lamp unto my feet and a light unto my path."[10]

Years ago I had a talk with one of the preachers at my church about the Bible. It seemed as though we had the same passion for the Word—neither one of us could get enough of it. I remember saying to him, "Our passion for the Lord seems to be at the same level. Maybe I am called to preach." That night the Lord set me straight. In a dream he stated: "I said teach the Word." Later, I went back to the same preacher and told him that God had not called me to preach. It is dangerous to try and perform duties that God has not called us to. The Word tells us King Saul lost his kingship because he performed a priestly duty that was not in line with his calling.[11] It is very important that you know your calling. My experience has proven that God can call us to different duties at different times during our life. In my lifetime I've sung, ushered, worked in missions and in evangelism. All of these capacities were important; they were all training ground for me to teach the Word.

My Call

On January 8, 1996, the Lord called me to the ministry. That particular night I was watching a video on the *Trinity Broadcasting System*. Bishop TD Jakes, one of the greatest preachers of our time, was preaching a sermon titled *Chosen to Change the Atmosphere.* I had seen this video several times before, but it was such an anointed message that I decided to watch it again. In fact, it was the second time TBN had shown it that particular week.

One of Bishop's main points was the importance of sacrifice, praise and worship. His presentation of the word was so dynamic; that I began to praise God at a level that I had never reached before. As I watched the video, I felt I was actually in the audience. I shouted out the highest praise (hallelujah) to the point where my chest began to hurt. As I praised the Lord, I kept falling to my knees. After a while I realized I was in the presence of the Holy Father.

Finally I asked, "What is it Lord?"

He said to me, "Preach the Word." And because I did not know many women preachers, I thought, *He must mean for me to pass this message along to my husband.* I said to Him, "Lord, you will have to send my husband to me so I can give him your message."

Soon after, my husband came down to the lower level of our home looking for me, but I could not say a word to him, nor he to me. I could not even look at him.

Eventually, he went back upstairs leaving me in privacy with the Lord. When the Lord finally released me, I told my husband what had transpired. Later, we decided that it would be best if I did not mention my experience to anyone. It was my husband's belief that if the Lord truly wanted me to preach his Word that he would bring the vision to pass.

In the months following I began to question my experience. It seemed as though the enemy was trying to make me doubt that God had really given me a promise, a vision, His purpose for my life. So the Lord reassured me several times that He truly did call me to preach his Word.

My first assurance came while I was traveling the streets of Detroit. While listening to the praises of God on the radio, the Lord began to say over and over in my spirit, "Preach the Word." He kept on saying it until I said, "Okay Lord, I hear you." The second time He reassured me by sending one of my mother's friends, whom I had not seen for several years, back into my life. At the time I thought, *Lord why would you call me to preach? There are no women preachers*. Needless to say, this woman was a preacher. She assured me I had indeed heard from the Lord. But after a while I began to question my calling again.

Finally, one night I decided to visit my sister's church. When the pastor preached, it seemed as though the sermon was tailored just for me.

The pastor said, "The Lord wants to know what He has to do to convince you that He really did say what you thought He said." I knew then the Lord was speaking directly to me. As the Word is preached, the Holy Spirit sends it to each individual in a way that benefits his or her life. As the word went forth, the preacher spoke into my life. That experience was the final convincing point.

Here I was called by God to preach his Word. I felt like the prophet Isaiah.

"Also I heard the voice of the Lord, saying, whom shall I send, and who will go for us? Then said I, Here am I send me."[12]

I thought, *how could I say no to the Lord? He has been so good to me. He saved, healed, delivered, and set me free.* So I said yes to his will and yes to his way.

I found that when the Lord calls, you need to say yes. In fact, you must say yes, if you don't you will be miserable like Jonah who ran from God's call. Don't worry about how or when He called you, just know that he did. No two calls are alike. Many people just hear the Lord speak into their hearts to preach the word, with no drama at all. But that does not make their experience any less genuine than one who the Lord calls in a dramatic way. So if the Lord calls you, just say "yes" and embrace the call. You will not be able to live the abundant life he promised until you say "yes" to him.

1. Job 14:1

2. Romans 10:17 "see also" Romans 10:9-10

3. 1 Corinthians 5:17

4. Romans 12:1-2

5. Peter 2:4

6. Jeremiah 1:5

7. Ephesians 1:4

8. 1 Peter 2:9

9. Psalms 24:1-2

10. Psalms 119:105

11. 1 Samuel 15

12. Isaiah 6:8

Chapter 2 - Don't Limit God

It was hard for me to believe that God chose or called me for His purpose. I thought, *why would the Lord choose me, I'm nobody*. I believed that most of the people the Lord chooses for his purpose are extraordinarily great people. I thought, *I am just an ordinary person. How can He use me in a ministerial capacity?*

In the days following, the Lord showed me He can use anybody. He also showed me several people in the Bible that He used in great ways, and people He is using in great ways today. These people probably felt ordinary as well. The Lord showed me the people I was comparing myself to were also ordinary until He changed them, gave them power, and prepared them for His service. As my pastor often says it isn't until God's *super* hits your *natural* that people are able to go great things for the Kingdom of God.

The Lord showed me that if we are going to work for Him we have to believe we are who He says we are. God has blessed His people. He has told us of His blessings in His word. We must have the faith to receive His blessings. If God tells you that you are great, then you are great. God tells us we are a "chosen generation, a royal priesthood, an holy nation, a peculiar people;

that ye should show forth the praises of Him who hath called you out of darkness into his marvelous light: which in time past were not a people, but are not the people of God: which had not obtained mercy, but now have obtained mercy."[1]

The people of God are royalty because we are the children of the great, high king.

> Lift up your heads, O ye gates: and be ye lifted up, ye everlasting doors: and the king of glory shall come in. Who is this King of Glory? The Lord strong and mighty, the Lord mighty in battle. Lift up your heads O ye gates: even lift them up, ye everlasting doors: and the king of glory shall come in. Who is the king of glory, The Lord of hosts, he is the King of glory, Selah.

> Psalm 24:7-10

God is the King of Glory. He is royalty and His words are true. So if God says you are royalty, you are royalty. If God says you are more than a conqueror, you are more than a conqueror. If He says you are victorious in Christ, you must believe Him. This is a spiritual thing, and I am talking spiritual principles. The word tells us God is a spirit, and we must worship in spirit and in truth.

You may feel as though you are a weak person. You may not think much of yourselves because of the circumstances that life has dealt you. But if you want to receive the promises of God you must change you way of thinking. You are better than your circumstances. If you want to move with God, you have to believe what He says.

You must have faith, and "faith comes by hearing, and hearing by the word of God."[2] Many people have low self-esteem.

This is primarily because of the belief systems they developed as a child. If we were degraded and discouraged, if we had controlling parents, we may not feel that we are good enough to be blessed.

———————

Some people feel they must have everyone's approval in order to survive. If they continue to hold to this belief, they will eventually make everyone their judge, and give away their power. Many believe that if someone does not like them, they are not loveable. These people tend to be people pleasers. They believe that if people disapprove of the actions they take, then their actions must be wrong. I have come to realize this belief is bound to make one depressed and frustrated.

"We have to know that people's opinions are not "the truth." They are only opinions, and opinions will differ on every subject."[3] The real truth is everyone is entitled to their own opinion. It's okay to listen to the opinions of others and take them into consideration, but we should not let them determine what we believe. We must affirm ourselves in God. We have to be independent of the approval of others, and know that we are the best judge of our own actions. We have to seek God for our every move. The Word tells us "the steps of a good man are ordered by the Lord; and he delighteth in his way."[4]

"Trust in the Lord with all thine heart: and lean not to thine own understanding, in all thy ways acknowledge Him, and He shall direct thy path."[5]

"If any man be in Christ, he is a new creature, old things are passed away, behold, all things have become new."[6]

We have to get rid of our old belief systems and acknowledge the word of the Lord for our lives. If we continue in these beliefs, we will not be able to accept the *great move* that God has for our life. We are chosen by God and He wants to lift us up. He wants *to do a new thing* in us.

———————

In Joshua 1, we are told that after watching their parents wander in the wilderness for forty years because of tradition and fear, the new generation of Israelites entered into the Promised Land. It is my belief they were ready to receive God's promise. I believe they did not want to miss the blessings that God had in store for them. However, God had to prepare both Joshua and the people by teaching them the importance of courageous and consistent faith. Before crossing the Jordan into the Promised Land, God gave the people new instructions for living because they had never been in that land before.

> So it was, after three days, that the officers went through the camp, commanding the people saying: when you see the ark of the covenant of the Lord your God, and the priest, the Levites, bearing it, then you shall set out from your place and go after it. Yet there will be space between you and it, about two thousand cubits by measure. Do not come near it that you may know the way by which you must go, for you have not passed this way before. If Joshua and the people of God had not followed God's instructions, they would not have seen the Promised Land, just like their parents.

Joshua 3:2-4

DON'T LIMIT YOURSELF

> Enlarge the place of thy tent, and let them
> stretch forth the curtains of thine habituations:
> spare not, lengthen thy cords, and strengthen
> thy stakes; for thou shall break forth on the
> right hand and on the left; and thy seed shall
> inherit the gentiles, and make the desolate
> cities to inhabited. Fear not, for thou shall not
> be ashamed: neither be thou confounded; for
> thou shall not be put to shame of thy youth,
> and shall not remember the reproach of thy
> widowhood any more.
>
> Isaiah 54:2-4

When God calls you to His service, know that you may have
to leave your comfort zone. You might have to leave some of
your friends. You might have to change churches. Whenever
He tells you to move, know that He has your best interest at
heart. Some friends are with you for a season, and some are for
a lifetime. The people and places that are currently in your life
may have given you all they can. They may not be able to take
to the level that God has for you.

If God tells you to move, you have to trust Him. If you do
not leave willingly, the Lord may make your surroundings
uncomfortable to encourage you to move on. Often times, we
won't move because we want to stay in familiar surroundings,
whether they are good or bad. We might think, *at least I know
who my enemies are right now!* That may be true, but are you
going to miss your blessing because of the familiar?

You have to encourage yourself. You have to keep moving in the direction God has shown you. Study the ministry. Surround yourself with people who are already in that particular ministry. God's plan for your life may be bigger than what you think it is!

"Be steadfast, unmovable, always abounding in the work of the Lord, for as much as ye know that your labor is not in vain."[7]

NOT EVERYONE WILL EMBRACE YOUR CALL

It's important to know other people might not want to embrace the vision, the call that God has given you. In fact, two weeks before the Lord actually called me to the ministry: the Lord showed me my calling in a dream. In the dream, my sister, another Christian, and I were in the middle of a rain storm. When the storm was over, and as the sky began to clear, my sister and I looked up and saw a beautiful newborn baby. It was so beautiful that we could only say, "My God!" Awestruck, we could only stair up at the sky. However, the other individual in my dream refused to even acknowledge the baby. Later the Lord showed me that the baby's birth symbolized the birth of my ministry. The baby symbolized that God was doing a "new thing" in my life.

Through this vision, the Lord was showing me not everyone was going to embrace what He was doing in my life. The other individual in my dream never acknowledged my calling. I really loved and respected this individual. It hurt me that she did not believe the vision God had given me, because she was a woman of spiritual wisdom. The enemy knew I really trusted this woman. He tried to convince me through her that God had not really called me. But I thank God He convinced me that His plan and purpose for me were real. Don't expect people to be with you in everything you do, especially if it involves promotion.

The Lord will give you dreams and visions years before they are to come to pass. But it is not always wise to share them with everybody because the devil might use them to put limits on you. For example, in Genesis 37:1-7, Jacob had a son in his old age named Joseph.[8] The Word tells us he treated Joseph with favoritism. He gave Joseph a fabulous coat of many colors, while his older brothers wore the attire of working shepherds.

The problem was Joseph had the habit of revealing dreams that predicted he would one day reign over his brothers. In fact, in one of his dreams, his sheaf of wheat stood upright as theirs gathered around and bowed down. Eventually his brothers became upset. One day when Joseph went out to the field, his brothers said, "Here comes this dreamer. Come let us kill him."[9] But the oldest brother objected to their plan. Instead, Joseph's brothers tore off his robe and threw him into a pit, and eventually sold him into slavery.

People might not believe your call. They might not believe the great things God has told you because He spoke them directly into your spirit. They might not believe the things God has shown you because all they see is your current position in life. Some might even believe the call, but they might not be able to adjust to it. They don't know God is going to take you through a transformation period.

I remember telling one of my closest friends the Lord had called me to preach.
"I don't think so," she said.

Had I listened to her, I would not have gone any further. But because I believed what the Lord spoke into my spirit, I was able to stand on His Word, and eventually I received His promise.

People will put limits on your calling; they will try to box you in. They will count you out of the game. But don't listen to people, listen to God. They don't know what God has told you. We can't let people impose limitations on us. We can't let people tell us that we can't do the things God has told us to do. The Word says, "I can do all things through Christ who has strengthened me."[10] So quit making excuses. Get up and do the will of God.

1. 1 Peter 2:9-10

2. Romans 10:17

3. Steven Farmer, M.A., M.F.C.C. *Adult Children of Abusive Parents.* New York, Ballantine Books, 1989. ISBN 0-345-36388-4

4. Psalms 37:23

5. Proverbs 3:5-6

6. 1 Corinthians 5:17

7. 1 Corinthians 15:58

8. Genesis 37:1-7

9. Genesis 37:19-20

10. Philippians 4:13

CHAPTER 3 – HOLD ON A MINUTE

There are many reasons why you may have to wait before going forth in your calling. I'm going to discuss two of these reasons.

The first reason you may have to wait has to do with your marital status. If God has called you into the ministry and you are a married woman, you must proceed with wisdom and caution.

"The wife is bound by the law as long as her husband liveth; but if her husband be dead, she is at liberty to be married to whom she will; only in the Lord."[1]

> But I want you to be without care. He who is unmarried cares for the things of the Lord – how he may please the Lord. There is a difference between a wife and a virgin. The unmarried woman cares about the things of the Lord, that she may be holy both in body and in spirit. But she who is married cares about the things of the world - how she may please her husband..."For the woman which hath an husband is bound by

law to her husband so long as he liveth: but if
the husband be dead, she is loosed from the law
of her husband."

1 Corinthians 7:32-34,39

Paul tells us that a single woman is free to do the things of the
Lord. He also states the unmarried person does better than the
married, meaning the single person has the potential of a greater
focus and time available for service to God and His work. The
single individual can serve the Lord with their whole heart.

Paul reminds us the married woman is subject to her husband.
Oftentimes, the husband may not be in agreement with God's
plan for his wife to preach the Word, or to pastor the Lord's people.
If you find yourself in this situation, your only responsibility is to
inform your husband of the instructions the Lord has given you
and leave it with Him. If he is not in agreement with the Lord's
plan, don't argue, don't fight, don't leave him or get a divorce. Just
pray. If you go to the Lord in prayer about the situation, in due
season, He will work it out. Just wait on the Lord. You may have
to wait a while for Him to pave the way. You may have to wait
a few days, a few months, or even years. You may see women go
forth in their ministry years before you do.

If these things happen, don't get upset. If you go ahead of the
Lord, you will ruin everything, may be even your marriage, and
that is not God's plan. You have to move when the Lord tells
you to and in the way He tells you to. However, you may have to
do a lot of fasting and praying beforehand.

"Is not this the fast that have chosen? to loose the bands of
wickedness, to undo the heavy burdens, and to let the oppressed
go free, and that ye break every yoke?"[2]

"Wait on the Lord be of good courage and, shall strengthen thine heart."[3]

I will repeat that again: Wait on the Lord! This is *his* doing. When the Lord wants you to move, you will be right on schedule. If you wait, oftentimes the Lord will change your husband's heart to the point where he is in approval of your ministry, and also one of your greatest supporters.

The second reason that you may have to wait has to do with your time spent with God. When you are devoted to reading God's Word, praying, fasting, and worshipping the Lord, He will elevate you in due season. He will take you to another level spiritually.

When you surrender your all to the Lord, when you make yourselves available to Him, when you are completely open to His will and to His way, the Lord will take you places that you have never seen before. He will open doors for you that you never thought you would walk through. In fact his Word says, "But it is written, eye hath not seen, nor ears heard, neither hath entered into the heart of man, the things which God hath prepared for them that love him."[4]

PEOPLE AND TRANSITION

If you are not careful, people will try to hold you back with their traditions. They may not be in agreement with the plans the Lord has for your life. However, the Lord does not always reveal to others the vision He has revealed to you regarding your life. Don't expect everyone to be in agreement with you because many are stuck in tradition. People who are stuck in traditional situations, in situations where they think God can only move in a particular way, might have some problems. God may reveal

His great secrets to them, but they may not acknowledge them because they have not seen God move in that particular way before.

Oftentimes I have heard people say, "We have always done things this way: my mother did it this way; my family has always done it this way; and this method of doing things has been passed down through my family line." Just because something has been done in a particular way for years, does not mean it can't be done another way. A particular method might have been right for a particular time, but it is not necessarily right for the season at hand.

People will talk about you when you try to escape the bonds of traditionalism. They will say you are a rebel and try to tear you down. Many will sit around watching and hoping that you will fail in your endeavor. But if you want to be in the will of God, you will have to ignore the negative talk and press on in the Lord. This may not be a comfortable time in your life. You may even feel that you are all alone. But remember God will never leave or forsake you.[5] It does not matter what people have to say; it is what God says that is important. Paul said: "For do I know persuade men or God? Or do I please man? For if I yet please men, I should not be the servant of Christ."[6] "If God be for us, who can be against us?"[7]

Don't let people bind you up in tradition. Christ has made you free. "Stand therefore in the liberty wherewith Christ hath made us free, and be not entangled again with the yoke of bondage"[8]

If we are bound to the former move of God, we will miss the new move, the new blessings that He has in store. And if we are not careful, people will try to hold us back with their traditions.

We can't get stuck in religious habits, thinking God will only work in specific ways.

It is nice to move in tradition in relation to worldly things, but when it comes to the things of God (spiritual things) we have to follow the Lord's instructions. God is not a God of tradition. He is a God of new thing.

"Behold, I will I do a new thing: now it shall spring forth: shall ye not know it? I will even make a way in the wilderness, and rivers in the desert."[9]

If we allow Him, He will order our steps according to His Word.

"The steps of a good man are ordered by the Lord: and he delighteth in his way. Don't let anyone hinder you from receiving your inheritance."[10]

"Beware lest anyone cheat you through philosophy and empty deceit, according to the *traditions of men*, according to the basic principles of the world, and not according to Christ."[11]

In this Scripture, Paul tells us to be careful of philosophies of life that are based only on human ideas and experiences. He condemns teaching that gives credit to men, and not to Christ. Men have their way of doing things, and God has his way. In Isaiah 55:8-9 we read, "For my thoughts are not your thoughts, neither are your ways my ways, saith the Lord. For as the heavens are higher than your ways, and my thoughts than your thoughts."[12]

Walking according to tradition will hinder the move of God in your life. If you find you are in a place where God is telling you to move in a specific direction, and it has been confirmed that you are really hearing from God, you can't let anyone hold you back. If you want to experience everything the Lord has for you,

you may have to leave the place of tradition, and you may have to leave complacent friends.

You may be in a place where you have been taught and trained for years. But after a while you may have to move because that particular place may not be able to take you to a higher level of learning. If you stay at that level, you will not experience the Lord's great blessings.

"Enlarge the place of thy tent, and let them stretch forth the curtains of thine habitations: spare not, lengthen thy cords, and strengthen thy stakes. For thou shall break forth on the right hand and on the left, and thy seed shall inherit the Gentiles, and make the desolate cities to be inhabited."[13]

1. 1 Corinthians 7:39

2. Isaiah 58:6

3. Psalms 27:14

4. 1 Corinthians 2:9

5. Hebrews 13:5

6. Galatians 1:10

7. Romans 8:31

8. Galatians 5:1

9. Isaiah 43:19

10. Psalms 37:23

11. Colossians 2:8, Italics added

12. Isaiah 55:8-9

13. Isaiah 54:2-3

Chapter 4 - The Process –
The Wait – Your Season Of Pain

After the Lord convinced me He truly *did* call me, I thought my work for Him would begin immediately. However, there were some things He needed to straighten out in my life before I could assume the position He promised. I thought about my shortcomings, my past sins, and thought, *How are you going to handle these matters, Lord?*

The prophet Isaiah had the same problem:

> In the year that king Uzziah died I saw also the Lord sitting upon a throne, high and lifted up, and his train filled the temple. Above it stood the seraphims: each one had six wings: with twain he covered his face, and with twain he covered his face, and with twain he did fly. And one cried unto another, and said, Holy, holy, holy, is the Lord of Hosts: the whole earth if full of his glory. And the posts of the door moved at the voice of him that cried, and the house was filled with smoke. Then I said, woe is me! For I am undone:

> Isaiah 6:1-5

After the Lord showed Isaiah His glory and holiness, Isaiah realized and admitted he was unclean, that he had sin in his life. He said in verse 5, "Woe is me! For I am undone: because I am a man of unclean lips and I dwell in the midst of a people of unclean lips: for mine eyes have seen the King, the Lord of hosts." Isaiah knew there were some things in his life the Lord needed to straighten out before he could serve him.

The Lord took care of Isaiah's concerns. A seraphim flew to him with a live coal in his hand, which he took with the tongs from off the altar, and he laid it upon Isaiah's mouth.

"And he said, 'Lo, this hath touch thy lips: and thine iniquity it taken away, and thy sin in purged.'"[1]

This was Isaiah's cleansing, consecration, purging period. Even though this process was painful for him, he had to go through it before he could truly serve the Lord. God cleansed Isaiah before giving him his assignment.

Like Isaiah, there were some sins and issues the Lord had to cleanse me of. If you are going to represent someone, you have to know that person and understand their ways; you have to be somewhat like them. After showing me His holiness, the Lord showed me some of the sins I had committed from childhood to adulthood. Like Isaiah, I thought *Lord, I am undone, a woman of unclean lips.* If you ask the Lord, He will forgive your sins, but there might be some residual thoughts, attitudes, and actions lingering in your life. The Lord must clean these things up, and He will put you through a cleansing process to do so.

The Lord must take all of us through His cleansing process. Like Isaiah, we all have to go through the fire. The Lord showed me that my baby (my ministry) could not be born until He had cleaned up the residue of my previous sins. When God is cleansing you, there is no doubt you are in the fire.

At one point, I shared with a senior pastor that I felt overwhelmed with what the Lord was doing. Things got so bad for me, I felt God had left me all alone.

"Barbara, you know how you always say 'the Lord is awesome?'" the pastor said. "Well He is awesome in every way (in salvation, healing, deliverance, transformation, in all that He does). Don't worry; God will never leave you nor forsake you."

One day I said to the Lord, "Things are really going bad; I don't understand what is going on. All I wanted to do was serve you. I just wanted to work for you. But I don't think I can go through with this. I have suffered so much and the price is so high. Lord, can we just forget about this whole thing?"

God then reminded me of the things that Jesus went through— the beatings, the scorning, the nails, the cross. I thought *Lord, how horrible. You didn't deserve any of that. I know that after you suffered, you received the name above all names. I just want to serve you in any way I can.*

The Lord replied, "If you want to work for Me and represent Me, you will have to suffer no matter what capacity you serve me in. I had to suffer, and you will to."

The Word says that the servant is not greater than his lord. Jesus said if He was persecuted, then we would be as well. [2]

He then told me, "If you suffer for my sake, you will also reign with Me."

No Cross, no crown.

In Hebrews 10:38 the writer states, "Now the just shall live by faith: but if any man draw back, my soul shall have no pleasure in him."

But hold on because Romans 8:18 says, "For I recon that the sufferings of this present time are not worthy to be compared with the glory which shall be revealed to us."[4]

You might be going through some terrible experiences right now. And you might be wondering what's going on. I submit to you the Lord might be taking you through the fire of purification for His service. If this is your situation, don't worry because God has said, "When you pass through the water, I will be with you. When you pass through the rivers, I won't let you drown."[5] When you walk through the fire he won't let you burn. You won't even smell of smoke.

"For I am the Lord your God, the Holy One of Israel. Fear not, for I am with thee, be not dismayed for I am thy God. I will strengthen you. I will help you. I will uphold you with the right hand of my righteousness."[6]

"My brethren, count it all joy when you fall into divers temptations: knowing this, that the trying of your faith worketh patience. But let patience have her perfect work, that ye may be perfect and entire, wanting nothing."[7]

"Beloved, think it not strange concerning the fiery trial which is to try you, as though some strange thing has happened to you: but in as much as ye are partakers of Christ's sufferings: that, when his glory shall be revealed, ye may be glad also with exceeding joy."[8]

You may be going through hard times, but God promises that He won't put you through anymore than you can bear.[9]

The Lord wants to burn off those things that are not of Him, so that you can be about His business. Understand that your fiery trials are just a test of the *Heavenly Development System.* There is no specific timetable for your season of trials, but be assured that when it is over, you will come forth as pure gold. Some unpleasant things might happen while you are in the fire, but take hold of God's promise.

"And we know that all things work together for good to them that love God, to them who are the called according to His purpose."[10]

When the Lord asked me, *Who will go for me? Who will be about my father's business?* I replied, "Here am I Lord, send me."

The Lord let me know that play time is over because He is coming back again. If I don't work for him, people will die in their sins, and I don't want their blood to be on my hands. I have to be about my Father's business and tell a dying world that Jesus lives, and because He lives, they can live also. The world needs to know that the wages (consequences) of sin is death, but the gift of God is eternal life through Jesus Christ our Lord.[11] I must proclaim that God loves the world so much He gave his only Son. And whoever believes on Him will have eternal life.[12] He has gone to prepare a place for all of us and where He is, we may be also.[13] The world needs to know that Jesus is coming back again—soon!

"If we confess our sins, that He is faithful and just to for give us of our sins and cleanse us from all unrighteousness."[14]

"Whosoever shall call upon the name of the Lord shall be saved."[15]

I must tell everyone one that if they confess with their mouth the Lord Jesus, and believe in their heart that God has raised him from the dead, they will be saved.[16]

"For with the heart man believeth unto righteousness and with the mouth confession is made unto salvation."[17]

I have to be about my Father's business, and so do you. Is there any one out there that the Lord can send? Who will go for Him? *God is calling you!*

1. Isaiah 6:6-7

2. John 15:20

3. Hebrews 10:38

4. Romans 8:18

5. Isaiah 43:2-3

6. Isaiah 41:10

7. James 1:2-4

8. 1 Peter 4:12-13

9. 1 Corinthians 10:13

10. Romans 8:28

11. Romans 6:23

12. John 3:16

13. John 14:3-13

14. 1 John 1:9

15. Romans 10:13

16. Romans 10:9

17. Romans 10:10

Chapter 5 –
Your Waiting Season

To every to every thing there is a season, and a time to every purpose under the heaven. A time to be born, and a time to die: a time to plant, and a time to pluck up that which was planted. A time to kill and a time to heal: a time to break down and a time to build up; A time to weep and a time to laugh; a time to morn, and a time to dance; A time to cast away stones, and a time to gather stones together; a time to embrace, and a time to reframe from embracing; a time to get, and a time to lose; a time to keep, and a time to cast away; A time to rend, and a time to sew; a time to keep silence, and a time to speak; A time to love, and a time to hate; a time of war, and a time of peace...I have seen the travail, which God hath given to the sons of men to be exercised of it. He hath made everything beautiful in his time: also he hath set the world in their heart, so that no man

can find out the work that God maketh from
the beginning to the end.

Ecclesiastes 3:1-8,10-11

God works in seasons with nature (winter, spring, summer, and
fall), and He works with us in the same manner. You might be
in the waiting season right now, which is your time of travail.
Just like a mother travails in the birth of her natural baby, you
must travail in the birth of your spiritual baby (the vision God
has given you).

During my waiting season, it seemed as though little or nothing
was happening in my ministry. I could feel my spiritual baby
kicking, trying to push forth. The Spirit of God was upon me
and I was ready for my vision to come to pass. However, just
as a woman in labor must resist pushing until it is time, I also
had to resist pushing the birth of my vision. Premature efforts
would have caused tearing and damage to both the vision and
myself.

A few special things happened to me during my waiting season.
First of all, my pastor at that particular time, preached one of
his anointed sermons titled *I'm getting ready for a major move*.
In his sermon, he described many of the experiences I was
having at that point in my life. He explained that if God has
proclaimed a promise over your life, you must do the following
to receive it:

- You must be obedient to the Lord.
- You must have the faith to receive it.
- You must prepare for it.
- You must focus on the future and not your current
  circumstances.

You must learn to praise the Lord before the move comes to pass. You must change your thinking processes (think major). Whether your "baby" is a new house, another degree, a business, a job—whatever the Lord is showing you, think major. The pastor stated we cannot be afraid and we must forget about our past sins order to receive the promise.

The second special thing that happened to me was I received an abundance of prophesies. Many of the Lord's ministers told me about the blessings, the vision the Lord had in store for my life. They told me about the things God had already placed in my spirit. Most of the prophecies were confirmations of visions or words the Lord had shown me or spoken to me over the years.

The Lord must remind us of His promises. Oftentimes He lets us know His plans or promises for our lives through our dreams. We think that they are just regular dreams that occur in our sleep. However, if you wait on the Lord, He will show you that they were not just regular dreams, but instead, future realities.

One day, a minister at my church prophesied to me. She told me things that God has in store for my life. She confirmed the things God had told me over the years, during my prayer time. A few times she gave me specific dates as to when my "move of God" was to take place. However, these prophesies did not come to pass when I thought they would. This upset me so much that I became confused, anxious, unsettled, angry and impatient. I knew she and the other people that prophesied to me were sincere, but somehow they had missed God. I was so upset that I had to pray fervently to get past my feelings. I was truly not myself.

By this time I had been through so much that I felt like saying

Lord let's just forget this whole thing, and I will just minister to the people that you send to me. I'm being hindered and held back for whatever reason. I even began to feel that some of the negative things people said about me were true—maybe I should not be preaching. In fact, my only engagement over the next two years was preaching in a small meeting for fifteen minutes. I thought *Lord I'm getting older and slowing down. When you bring me into the vision, the blessings that you have shown me, I will be too tired to enjoy or handle them.*

Up to that point I had to put a great deal of effort into all of the assignments that were given to me. I tried to be faithful in everything, but it seemed as though my efforts were unappreciated. It also seemed as though many people were placed in positions over me who were younger and less experienced than me.

I began to earnestly pray and seek the Lord for peace in the situation. I had to go boldly to the throne of grace to obtain mercy and find grace to help in the time of need.[1]

One night at Bible study, my pastor was teaching on *The Transition Position.* During his teaching, he described the feelings I was experiencing. He explained that in order to get to the next level, in order to receive the blessings of God, one must go through transition.

During the message, the Lord revealed to me He was working behind the scenes, making preparations for His plans to come to past in my life. During my down times, He was preparing me for the blessings He had promised. God was giving me small opportunities to minister in ways other than preaching during the church services. He was perfecting me and stirring up my gifts. He was also testing my faith to see if I would trust

Him to bring the vision to pass, and to see if I would continue to praise and worship Him while I waited.

In the waiting season, your baby—your vision—is in the birthing position. During this time the enemy will send all types of distractions, trying to abort your promise because he does not want it to materialize. But you have to put the devil under your feet and wait on the Lord.[2]

After reading the Word, I began to calm down. I remembered this whole plan was the Lord's, not mine. I realized that if God did not step in, the vision would not come to pass. I thought, *the Lord is teaching me patience and maturing me.* I remembered Philippians 1:6, "Being confident of this very thing, he which hath begun a good work in you will perform it until the day of Jesus Christ."[3]

"But the God of all grace, who hath called us unto His eternal glory by Christ Jesus, after that ye have suffered a while, make you perfect, stablish, strengthen and settle you."[4]

Make no mistake: your faith will be tried.

"The trying of your faith worketh patience. But let patience have her perfect work, that ye may be perfect and entire, wanting nothing."[5]

Be patient and be faithful. If you are in a season of waiting, don't push until God says push. I'm talking in the spirit now. Doctors tell us a woman in labor is in so much pain that she just wants the baby out. And if she does not have a coach, she will push too soon, and can hurt herself and endanger the child. When you are in the waiting season, the pain might be intense, but hold on. Don't let anything or anyone allow you to push ahead of time.

You have to enter into the rest of the Lord. The Word tells us that we must mix our faith with the promises God had given us. Positioning involves little physical movement, and a lot of spiritual warfare.

You must be steadfast, unmovable; always abounding in the work of the Lord, for as much as ye know that your labor is not in vain in the Lord.[6] You must firmly resist any temptation to quit. I know it is hard to wait, and sometimes even harder to wait on the Lord. But you have to remember that your vision is the Lord's doing. You have to wait on Him, because He has the plan *and* the schedule.

Remember, God is omniscient, omnipotent, omnipresent, and sovereign (all knowing, has all power, everywhere at all times, and He can do what ever He wants to do, when He wants to). You have to be like King David: Wait on the Lord and be of good courage. If you wait, the Lord will strengthen your heart. Follow His plan and keep busy doing the things that will increase your knowledge and experience in the area of your calling, such as studying God's Word and taking ministry classes.

You have to realize the greater the vision the Lord gives you, the greater the test and training. You must realize that to whom much is given, much is required. Take the prophesies that are given to you with a grain of salt: appreciate them, but put them on a shelf in the back of your mind.

> Cast not away therefore your confidence, which
> hath recompense of reward. For ye have need
> of patience, that after ye have done the will of

God, ye might receive the promise. For yet a little while, and he that shall come will come, and will not tarry. Now the just shall live by faith, but if any man draw back, my soul shall have no pleasure in him.

Hebrews 10:35-38

I know that you may have been through all of the seasons (winter, spring, summer, and fall); and you had to weather the storms. I know that you have been tested and tried, but it is through these trying experiences that the Lord teaches us His battle strategies. The Lord will show you what you should and should not do.

If your baby is in the birth canal and you have been travailing, hold on because, "if God be for you, *who* can be against you?"[7]

Beware of the distractions the enemy puts in your way to get you out of position. Beware of distractions that stir you up, that cause you to draw apart, that cause confusion and have conflicting emotions. Stay focused.

"And let us not grow weary in well doing, for in due season we shall reap if we faint not"[8]

1. Hebrews 4:16.

2. Ephesians 1:22

3. Philippians 1:6

4. 1 Peter 5:10

5. James 1:3-4

6. 1 Corinthians 15:58

7. Romans 8:31

8. Galatians 6:9

CHAPTER 6 -
THE SHIFT - (TRANSITON,
ELEVATON, COMPLETION)

If the Lord has given you a vision, you must wait for Him to bring it to pass. If you can develop it on your own, it may be a good idea but not necessarily a God idea. A true vision from God requires revelation by His Spirit. He has to provide direction for the vision. A true vision does not come about right away. You will experience a lot of waiting between the time the Lord shows you the vision and its birth. I have discovered that the Lord teaches us patience through waiting.

At the beginning of the year, my pastor gave the congregation three words to focus on: *transition, elevation, and completion.* As we know, seven is the number of completion in God's kingdom. It was the October, 2007, the year of completion. And it appeared as though nothing was happening in relation to my vision. However, my church completed its building process, and we were scheduled to move into the new building on the 7th.

Every week my pastor preached messages that related to transition, elevation, and completion. These messages were not only for the church as whole, but for each member individually. The pastor stated there was still three months left in the year in which the Lord could still do some great things in our lives.

Even though I received many prophecies in relation to what the Lord was about to do with my ministry, doubt began to set in. There were days I thought the things that happened in relation to my ministry were my imagination. Oftentimes I had to remind myself the Word of God tells us to walk by faith, not by sight.

I was seeing other individuals going forth in their ministries, but I wasn't seeing any real movement in mine. Each day seemed like more of the same. While waiting for the promise (the vision), it is easy to get excited because of the anticipated blessing.

One day, I went to the health spa to work out. While I was resting in between workout sessions, a woman came over to me and began to talk about spiritual matters. I realized she was a woman of God, one whom He used prophetically. This woman began to pray for me and to speak into my life.

There are times the vision takes so long to materialize the Lord will send a prophet(ess) to remind you of His promise, and encourage you to hold on.

This woman said to me, "I don't know who you are, but God is about to do some great things in your life."

Everything the woman said was a confirmation of what God had already told me. Finally, she prayed for me and told me I was blessed. I knew this was truly of God because she had never seen me before, but her message was accurate.

A week later the Lord gave me a sermon titled *The Shift*. The scriptures are found in I Samuel 10:1-25.

Chapter 10 opens up with Samuel anointing Saul as king of Israel. Historically, when an Israelite took office, it was customary for him to be crowned and anointed with oil. While Saul was out looking for his father's donkeys, Samuel surprised him by sharing God's vision for his life, and anointing him for his kingly position.

The Lord will surprise you by giving you a vision for your life as well. The purpose of the vision is to make your life joyful, fulfilling, and meaningful. A vision is a gift from God. It is his way of letting us be a part of his kingdom building. The Word tells us that we must have a vision, because without it we will perish.[1]

Samuel anointed Saul as the first king of Israel. However, Saul did not sit in the kingly seat right away; he had to go through a refining process. He had to follow the instructions the Lord gave Samuel for his ministry in order to receive his promise.

When God gives you a vision it may not come to pass right away. It may months or even years. The Lord may delay the vision in order to prepare you for your next level. You have to go through several tests, trials, and experiences before God can bring the vision to pass. You will have to go through a refining process.

Samuel gave Saul specific instructions.

"When you leave me, you will run into two men. And these men will tell you that the donkeys you are looking for have been found."[2]

In verse 3, Samuel told Saul he would meet into three other men, carrying three goats, three loaves of bread, and a wine skin. Verse 5 states Samuel told Saul that after entering the city, he would come across a group of prophets returning from a prayer meeting. They would be carrying a stringed instrument, a tambourine, a flute, and a harp. They would also be prophesying. From these verses we learn that God gave Saul specific instructions through the man of God. He told him what to look for ahead of time, so he would not be misguided. When God gives you a vision, he will also give you instructions. If you are obedient to him, one day you will receive the promise.

In verses 6 and 7 Samuel gave Saul further instructions. He told Saul that after the prophets spoke into his life, the Spirit of the Lord would come upon him. He would prophesy with them, and then be turned into another man. In other words, *a shift* was about to take place in Saul's life. The Spirit of the Lord would come upon him and the vision would come to pass.

The Lord began to show me how this portion of Scripture related to my situation. Allow me to explain. Three weeks before we were to move into our new church building, a young lady I worked with told me the Lord woke her up in the night and gave her an assignment to introduce me to her mother, a pastor.

A month later, I spoke with her mother on the telephone. At the end of the conversation, her mother prayed for me and spoke into my life. She confirmed many of the things the Lord had already told me. The next day my friend and I rejoiced over the conversation because we knew it was from the Lord. As we walked out of the office, she said, "Barbara, the Lord said in thirty days he is going to do something great in your life. I see an explosion over you."

She saw an explosion of God's Glory, of him changing me into the person I needed to be to do all of the things He showed me in the vision, just as happened to Saul. An elevation was about to take place.

She said, "Barbara, I am so happy for you. Get ready, get ready, get ready."

Needless to say that was a shocking experience.

As I was walking one Saturday morning, the Lord let me know He was about to move me to a new place. He reminded me I was not going to be a member of my current church much longer. He said I was there mainly for preparation and training. I was surprised, because I thought I would there for a long time. At that point I began to reflect on the past.

When the Lord is about to bring you into your calling, the enemy will get busy. He will remind you of the people who made you promises, but did not follow through. He will replay in your mind all of the bad things you went through during your refining process. He will whisper the names of those who hurt you, left you, who talked about you, who discounted and doubted you. He will remind you that you expected certain people to help you with your ministry. Even though you were faithful to them, they did not come through for you. If you pay attention to him, you will become bitter.

The Lord showed me that order for him to do a new thing in my life, in order for him to bring the vision to pass; I could not let the devil distract me. He let me know that I had to do as the Word says.

"Let all bitterness, and wrath, and anger, and clamor, and evil speaking, be put away from you, with all malice: and be kind to one another, tenderhearted, forgiving one another, even as God for Christ's sake have forgiven you."[3]

I had to do these things in order to receive God's promise.

That Sunday, the last Sunday in the church's old location, the Lord confirmed His Word. My pastor preached from Philippians:

"Brethren, I count not myself to have apprehended; but this one thing I do, forgetting those things which are behind, and reaching forth unto those things which are before, I press toward the mark for the prize of the high calling of God though Christ Jesus."[4]

In order to move into my calling, I had to press through the enemy's distractions. I had to forgive. I had to think on the good things that happened during my refining process. I had to thank the Lord for the people who gave me the opportunity to do some of the things that related to my ministry, no matter how small the opportunities. I began to praise the Lord for those individuals, and to ask Him to bless them in all their endeavors. Soon I began to feel free and ready for the next move of God.

Opening day of our new sanctuary was awesome. The Spirit of God met us in the new building in mighty way. During the service, I sat with three of the ministers whom the Lord uses greatly in the prophetic. They began to prophesy to me regarding my ministry, and about becoming a pastor of my own church. They told me the Lord was about to bestow great blessings in my life. They also explained how the enemy would try to hinder God's plans.

Later, the Lord had me prophesy to them regarding some things in their lives. The whole situation reminded me of I Samuel 10. The word *shift* kept coming up in sermons and conversations, and I knew the Lord was about to do something.

As the year was coming to an end, I thought *when is the Lord going to do all of the things that have been prophesied? The year is almost over. I know the people who prophesied to me are legitimate, so what's going on?* I was very discouraged. *Lord, I am getting older. I'm slowing down, and have not received the training that is needed to do all of the things you have said. There are only a few more days left before the year is out. It was prophesied I would complete some things this year. 2007 is a year of transition, elevation and completion. I do not see any of these things happening in my personal life.*

The following Sunday my pastor accepted an assignment at another church, so his wife preached. That was a blessing, because his wife is filled with the Spirit. She is great preacher in her own right.

She preached from Lamentations:

"The Lord is my portion, saith my soul; therefore will I hope in Him".[5]

In her message she said, "Many of you have received prophecies this year. Earlier in the year many of the visiting ministers had prophesied to the church as a whole. They explained that before the year was over, the Lord was going to do great things in the lives of several of the church members."

The pastor's wife said, "The year is almost over and none of the prophesies have come to pass. You are probably thinking they were not of God. I want you to know there are still twenty-two days left in the year and God is still going to move in a mighty way. So don't lose hope: Just wait on the Lord."

She stated all of the things that were prophesied to us before the year was out were still going to come to pass. As she spoke, the Spirit of the Lord took over the remaining portion of the service. From that point the Lord began to send people to me regarding my shift to the new church. These people did not know anything about my vision. I believe the Lord was trying to encourage the entire congregation because we all jumped to our feet and praised Him. I thought, *Okay Lord, I still believe you.*

I went to Bible college that Monday night as I always did, and the instructor closed out class by saying, "I believe the Lord is going to do some great things in your lives before the year is over."

At that point I began to thank the Lord for responding to my prayers.

The first Sunday in November, my friend's mother and I spoke on the telephone. We talked about the things the Lord was currently doing in my life, and the things He was about to do. We both realized the Lord was about to shift me to her church so that she could prepare me for my own congregation. In fact, He had already given her the plan. It was her belief that she was to mentor me for my position as a pastor. As she shared the plan the Lord had given her for my ministry, I began to pray. I was supposed to call my friend's mother after I heard from the Lord regarding the matter.

The following Wednesday, I went to Bible study and the Lord confirmed the plan through my pastor. During the study session he said to the congregation, "Some of you are just one phone call, just one email away from your destiny."

I thought *Lord if this is truly your plan; it would truly be a Major Move.* The Lord reminded me of the prophetic message the pastor preached at the beginning of the year titled *Major Move.*

After the sermon he explained the Lord was about to move greatly in the lives of several of His people. He began to lay hands on those whom the Lord was going to move, including me. That was the convincing point for me. After praying about the situation, I realized this was the Lord's doing, and it was marvelous in my sight. I informed my co-worker's mother, I was going to follow through with the Lord's plan.

Later, I had a moment of unbelief. I began to think I was making a mistake. Was this truly God? Was I just being anxious? I had gone to a service that November where my nephew was ordained as an elder and a few ministers were also being ordained as pastors. I began to search my heart. Was I dreaming everything up because I wanted to be like the other ministers, or was this truly God? The Lord kept assuring me it was truly my season, my time of elevation.

Unfortunately a few of my close friends did not believe I had heard from the Lord. They did not believe the Lord could use me in that manner. I learned that you cannot share everything with everyone. You have to do what the Lord tells you to do, whether people believe you or not. The Lord gave you the vision, not them. It hurts to know that people don't believe the Lord can use you in a mighty way, but you have to get over it. You have to set your face like a flint and press on in Jesus.

THE RELEASE

As time went by, my friend's mother kept reassuring me this was a move of God, and the Lord kept sending people to me with a word of reassurance. Eventually, I went to the pastor and to tell him what the Lord said and to ask for a release. After the pastor and I discussed the matter he told me that I was released. There is a proper way to leave a church. It is best to leave with the pastor's blessing, and give your spiritual leader the respect he or she deserves. Leaving in this manor allows you to remain in the will of God.

On New Years Eve, I decided to go to my husband's church. I wanted to bring in the New Year with him. However, my mind was really at my church because I felt that my pastor was going to speak a word that related to my move. The following Sunday I purchased the CD of the New Years Eve service.

The pastor preached a message a message titled *There is a Release*.

"Many of you are not sure of what your future holds, but you are sure of who holds your future," he said. "This is a destiny moment for some of you. This year is going to be different because you have been released."

He stated the Lord allowed us to complete some things in 2007, in order that we might be released in 2008 for our new beginnings.

The pastor's message came from Deuteronomy:

> At the end of every seven years thou shalt
> make a release. And this is the manner of the
> release: every creditor that lendeth ought unto
> his neighbor shall release it; he shall not exact
> it of his neighbor, or his brother; because it is
> called *the Lord's release*. At the end of every
> seven years thou shalt make a release. And this
> is the manner of the release; every creditor that
> lendeth ought unto his neighbor shall release
> it; he shall not exact it of his neighbor, or his
> brother, because *it is called the Lord's release*.
>
> Deuteronomy 15:1-2, Italics added

The pastor said, "We are here tonight at the end of seven years, and there is to be a release. 2008 is a leap year, and if you need a release just leap for it. The seven years is up and a release is on the way. There are individuals here who are about to be released from a stressful period in their lives. These people are at the end of frustration, disappointment, discouragement, and bad relationships. The Lord is about to replace these situations with new and great situations. He is using 2007 to help get some things to these people, and to release them into a new realm of consciousness (about the things of God)."

The pastor stated the number seven represents completion; the number eight represents new beginnings.

"We have already completed everything that we needed in order to go into our new beginning. This message is not just for the individuals to whom God was talking to now, but it's also a way for these people to help others obtain their release."

He went on to explain that at this point in our lives we are about to have a "David experience." We were about to recover everything that the devil has stolen from us.[6]

"The Lord is about to release some people, and to take them to another place in Him. He is about to give them a new start, a new direction, and a new anointing. Some of you have been released. *This is the Lord's release.*"

That was a convincing point for me. I had truly been released to move on to the next phase of my ministry.

The first Sunday in January, my pastor preached a message titled "Its Your Time to Shine." The scriptures regarding the message are found in Isaiah.

> Arise, shine; for thy light is come, and the glory of the Lord is risen upon thee, for, behold, the darkness shall cover the earth, and gross darkness the people: but the Lord shall rise upon thee, and his glory shall be seen upon thee. And the Gentiles shall come to thy light, and the kings to the brightness of thy rising.
>
> Isaiah 60:1-3

> Violence shall no more be heard to thy land, wasting nor destruction with in thy borders; but thou shall call thy walls Salvation; and thy gates Praise. The sun shall be no more thy light by

day; neither for brightness shall the moon give light unto thee: but the Lord shall be unto thee an everlasting light, and thy God thy glory.

The sun shall no more go down; neither shall thy moon withdraw itself: for the Lord shall be thine everlasting light, and the days of thy mourning shall be ended.

Thy people also shall be all righteous; they shall inherit the land for ever, the branch of my planting, the work of my hands, that I may be glorified. A little one shall become a thousand and a small one a strong nation: I the Lord will hasten it in his time.

Isaiah 60:18-22

The pastor continued. "It's your time to shine. No more depression, sadness, or darkness. In the past, you have been there for other people, helping them with their problems. You have put your assignment on hold in order that you might help them fulfill their dreams. But it's your time to shine now. God released you last year to shine for Him this year.

"People will not understand why you can't spend all of your time with them, and do for them as you have in the past. They need to know this year you will be spending your time working on the promise the Lord has given you. This is not the year for you to be following in the shadows of other people. God says, 'arise in the things that I have given you to do.' It is time to use the light the Lord has put in you. Its time to stand up and do what the Lord told you to do. Matthew 5:16 says, "Let your light so shine before men, that they may see your good works, and glorify your Father which is in heaven.""

"You will not just be shining for yourself because everything the Lord has for you has a kingdom purpose. Your shining is going to attract resources in your direction. It will attract the right people at the right time for the right place in your life. It's time to make room for some new people in your life. People that have hindered you in the past, people that take away from you will have to go."

The pastor stated that it is time for us to get a "rising mind set." It's time to set our minds on things above. It is time to refuse things that don't take us to another level.

"It is time for you to remind yourself of the great things God has in store for you. Arise because the circumstances that have darkened you have passed. This year you will know why some people have treated you badly. God is taking you to another wave of glory. He must make you uncomfortable in order for you to move. God's glory is going to shine and you will have clarity in what you are to do, the steps you are to take. God is releasing glory into your life. His glory is about to shine and rest upon you. His glory is going to be your answer to the darkness that is around you. God's glory is going to be seen on you. Other people will forget about darkness and head toward the light that is in you. You are about to change the atmosphere because the light of His glory is shining on you."

He continued by saying people (unbelievers) will be attracted to us, so we have to look like Jesus. People will realize there will be no more foolishness because the glory of Lord will be in the atmosphere when we enter the room. He stated the Gentiles shall come into our lives. People who normally would not give us the time of day are going to be used by God to bring favor in our lives. People are going to be drawn to us. The kings of society, business, and government will take notice of our brightness and we will receive special blessings.

"You have fasted, prayed, and sought God, so kings will be coming your way. God is going to use these people to bless you. You have been down and discouraged for too long. You have taken the weight of other people's problems on your shoulders, but now it is time for you to shine. God has allowed His glory to illuminate your pathway. You will be free this year to release what God has put in you. This is your time to rise up and shine. This is the year for you to be happy. This is your year for supernatural release, and supernatural progress. Arise and shine because His glory has come upon you."

I realized that on New Years Eve the pastor had released me to my new beginnings, my church of preparation, and into the next phase of my ministry. On the first Sunday of 2008, blessings were given in relation to "the move." The Lord's release had come to pass. It was finished, the major move, the shift had taken place. I felt anxious, but I kept moving because I knew the Lord was with me.

"What can we say to these things? If God be for us, who can be against us?"[7]

1. Proverbs 29:18.

2. 1 Samuel 10:2

3. Ephesians 4:31-32

4. Philippians 3:13-14

5. Lamentations 3:24

6. 1 Samuel 30:1-20

7. Romans 8:31

CHAPTER 7 –
THE NEW BEGINNING

I began the New Year at my new church. Shortly after moving there, the pastors (husband and wife) ordained me as an associate pastor. They also placed me over the church's Board of Education. Everything had changed. It no longer mattered to me what people thought about my move, because I knew it was of God.

While all of these changes were taking place I became a mother-in-law and a grandmother. I was also in college pursuing my Doctorate of Divinity, and writing this book. The Lord kept me very busy. The Lord uses busy people. I didn't know I was going to do all of these things, but I knew I had to do everything the Lord told me to do, and I had to do them in His timing.

Timing is everything.

I realize that everything I have done and will do is preparation for my position as a pastor. The Lord will give strength in relation to his purpose.

Just as Joshua served and trained under Moses' leadership, I am now serving and training under my pastors. It now appears the Lord is about to do another shift in my life. It appears he is about to give me a congregation of people to shepherd. I believe this shift is about to take place because the Lord continues to bring the book of Joshua to my attention.

After the death of Moses the servant of the Lord it came to pass, that the Lord spake unto Joshua the son of nun, Moses' minister, saying, Moses my servant is dead; now go over this Jordan, thou, and all this people, unto the land which I give to them, event to the children of Israel.

Every place that the sole of your foot shall tread upon, that have I given unto you, as I said unto Moses. From the wilderness and this Lebanon even unto the great river, the river Euphrates, all the land of the Hitites, and unto the great sea toward the going down of the sun, shall be your coasts.

There shall not any man be able to stand before thee all the days of thy life; as I was with Moses, so I will be with thee: I will not fail thee, nor forsake thee.

Be strong and of good courage; for unto this people shalt thou divide for an inheritance the land, which I sware unto their fathers to give them. Only be thou strong and very courageous, that thou mayest observe to do according to all the law, which Moses my servant commanded thee; turn not from it to the right hand or to the left, that thou mayest prosper whithersoever thou goest.

This book of the law shall not depart out of thy mouth; but thou shalt meditate therein day and night, that thou mayest observe to do according to all that is written therein: for then thou shalt make thy way prosperous, and then thou shalt have good success. Have not I commanded thee? Be strong and of a good courage; be not afraid, neither be thou dismayed; for the Lord thy God is with thee whithersoever thou goest.

Joshua 1:1-9

One Sunday my pastor preached on these verses. The following week the Lord brought the same passage of Scripture to my attention as I was out for my daily walk. The next Wednesday the pastor spoke on the same Scriptures again. Later, we had a conversation and I believe the Lord informed her that He is preparing me for another shift.

We discussed the scriptures from Joshua 1. The pastor explained that in my case, the death of Moses represented the death of bad situations, discouragement, disappointments, and other things that were holding me back. God was about to shift me into my promised position, the vision, that he had given me twelve years ago.

She said, "Rise up from morning the loss of old things and prepare yourself to receive the new things God has for you. God's promise to you, your destiny is about to come to forth."

I am apprehensive. I don't know how the Lord is going to do all He has said, but I do know He is with me. The Lord reassured me I don't have to worry because He has everything under control. He also reminded me of a message that was preached by my previous pastor. It was titled "The Impossible is Still Possible" from the book of Luke.

> And in the sixth month the angel came Gabriel was sent from God into a city of Galilee, named Nazareth. To a virgin espoused to a man whose name was Joseph, of the house of David; and the virgin's name was Mary.

> And the angel came in unto her, and said, Hail, thou that art highly favored, the Lord is with thee: blessed art thou among women.

> And when she saw him, she was troubled at his saying, and cast in her mind what manner of salutation this should be. And the angel said unto her, fear not, Mary; for thou hast found favor with God. And, behold, thou shalt conceive in thy womb, and bring forth a son, and shalt call his name Jesus.

> He shall be great, and shall be called the Son of the Highest; and the Lord shall give unto him the throne of his father David; And he shall reign over the house of Jacob for ever; and of his kingdom there shall be no end. Then Mary said unto the angel, how can this be, seeing I know not a man?

> And the angel answered and said unto her, The Holy Ghost shall come upon thee and the power of the Highest shall overshadow thee: therefore also that holy thing which shall be born of thee shall be called the Son of God. And, behold, thy cousin Elizabeth, she hath also conceived a son in her old age: and this is the sixth month

with her, who was called barren. For with God
nothing shall be impossible.

Luke 1:26-37

The pastor explained that when God told Mary she was going
to have a child, she asked how it could be possible. He related
this to our modern day situations.

"Perhaps God has been telling you the things that He wants to
do through you, but you are looking at yourself as Mary looked
at herself, asking, 'how will this be?' You may be thinking, *I
don't have the training, the connections, or the skill to accomplish
these things.* Like Mary, you are thinking in the natural, that
you must have man's help to do them. The scriptures tell us
God's answer to Mary was, "The Holy Ghost shall come upon
thee.'"

The pastor stated the Holy Spirit can impregnate us with a
vision, inspire us with creative ideas, introduce us to the right
people, and empower us to do the job. The message the angel
gave to Mary still stands today, "for nothing is impossible with
God." We can be confident that God has begun a good work
us.[1] If the Lord gives you a vision, a promise, you can be assured
he will bring it to pass in your life.

> Wherefore seeing we also are compassed about
> with so great a cloud of witnesses, let us lay
> aside every weight, and the sin which doth so
> easily beset us, and let us run with patience the
> race that is set before us. Looking to Jesus the
> author and finisher of our faith; who for the
> joy that was set before him endured the cross,
> despising the shame, and is set down at the
> right hand of the throne of God. For consider
> him that endured such contradiction of sinners

against himself, lest ye be wearied and faint in
your minds.

Hebrews 12:1-3

Your ministry preparation will not be exactly like mine, but
you will have similar experiences. If you want to receive the
promise the Lord has given you, be obedient to Him as you go
your own refining process.

1. Philippians 1:6